# USBORNE BIG MACHINES
# RACING CARS

## Clive Gifford

### Designed by Robert Walster

### Illustrated by Chris Lyon

Additional illustrations by Andy Burton, Mark Franklin and Sean Wilkinson
Cover design by Tom Lalonde

Consultant: Quentin Spurring (Editor, Racecar Engineering)

## Contents

# Touring car racing

Ever since the first cars were made, people have raced them against each other. There are now many different types of racing. You can find out about them in this book.

## Touring cars

Touring cars are like ordinary road cars. They don't race on roads, though - they speed around a special racing track.

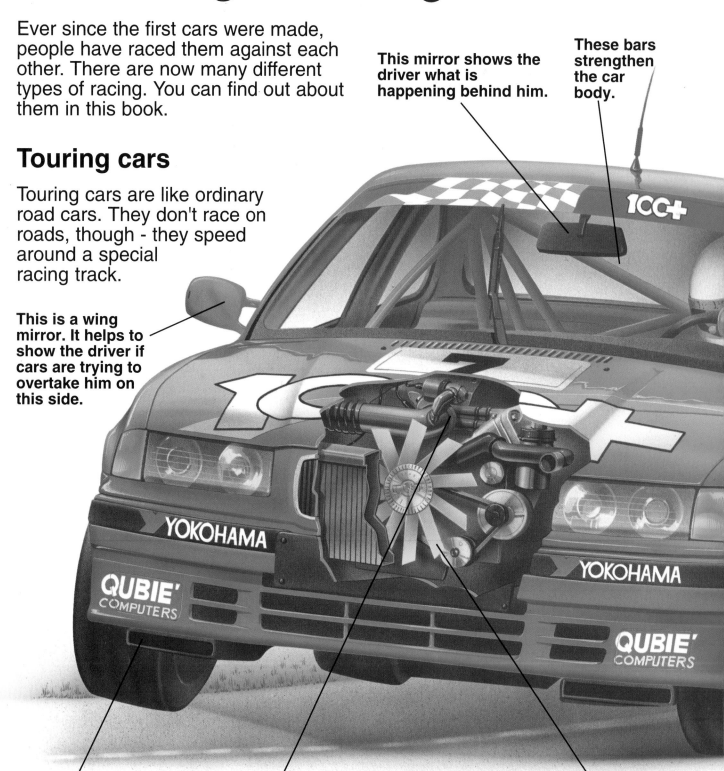

**This mirror shows the driver what is happening behind him.**

**These bars strengthen the car body.**

**This is a wing mirror. It helps to show the driver if cars are trying to overtake him on this side.**

**The car goes so fast around corners that sometimes two wheels can lift off the ground.**

**Touring cars can race at speeds up to 275km/h (170 mph).**

**Here you can look inside the car at the engine. Touring car racers often use the car's normal engine.**

**Sometimes, a more powerful engine is put in. This makes the car go even faster.**

**As the car races, the engine gets hot. This fan helps cool it down.**

**Touring car races can be very exciting. In most races the cars drive very close to each other.**

**Drivers always wear crash helmets (see below).**

## Safety clothing

Driving a racing car can be dangerous. Drivers protect themselves by wearing special clothes.

**This is called a balaclava. It is fireproof and protects the driver's face.**

**The racing suit fastens tightly at the neck.**

**All of the driver's clothes are fireproof.**

**The gloves help stop fire from burning his hands. They are often called gauntlets.**

**The special boots are very light. They are also fireproof.**

## Crash helmets

Racing drivers must protect their heads in case they crash. A crash helmet stops the head from getting badly hurt.

**The see-through part of the helmet at the front lifts up. It is called a visor.**

# Grand Prix cars

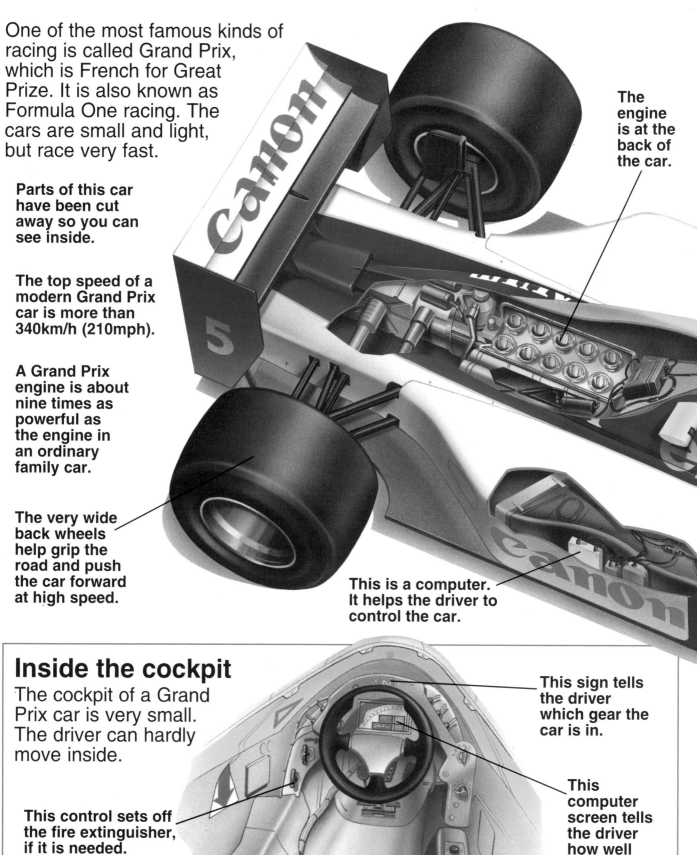

One of the most famous kinds of racing is called Grand Prix, which is French for Great Prize. It is also known as Formula One racing. The cars are small and light, but race very fast.

**Parts of this car have been cut away so you can see inside.**

**The top speed of a modern Grand Prix car is more than 340km/h (210mph).**

**A Grand Prix engine is about nine times as powerful as the engine in an ordinary family car.**

**The very wide back wheels help grip the road and push the car forward at high speed.**

**The engine is at the back of the car.**

**This is a computer. It helps the driver to control the car.**

## Inside the cockpit

The cockpit of a Grand Prix car is very small. The driver can hardly move inside.

**This control sets off the fire extinguisher, if it is needed.**

**This sign tells the driver which gear the car is in.**

**This computer screen tells the driver how well the engine is running.**

## Car cam

A tiny camera is fitted to some cars. This takes exciting pictures of the view from the cockpit. The film is often shown on television.

`0:55.72 79 MPH`

This shows the car's speed.

This shows how long the car has been racing.

This wing mirror shows how close cars are behind.

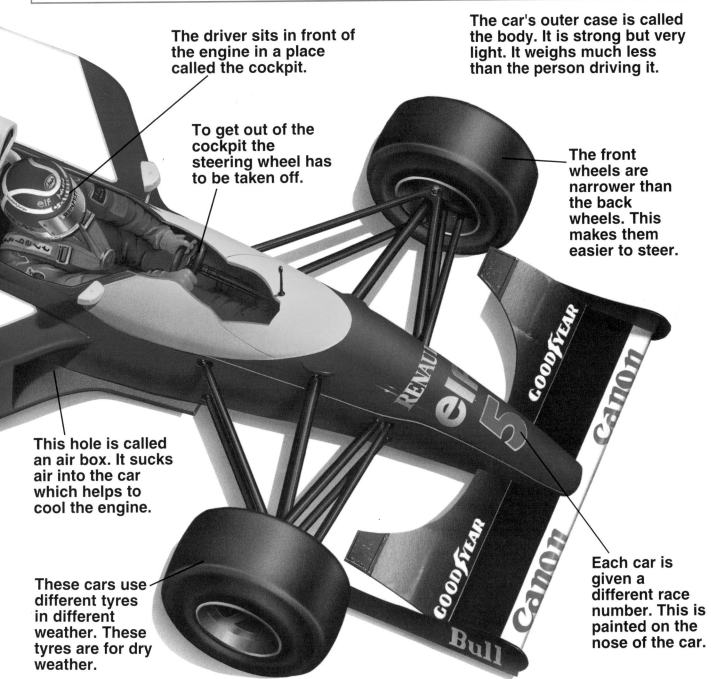

The driver sits in front of the engine in a place called the cockpit.

To get out of the cockpit the steering wheel has to be taken off.

The car's outer case is called the body. It is strong but very light. It weighs much less than the person driving it.

The front wheels are narrower than the back wheels. This makes them easier to steer.

This hole is called an air box. It sucks air into the car which helps to cool the engine.

These cars use different tyres in different weather. These tyres are for dry weather.

Each car is given a different race number. This is painted on the nose of the car.

# At the track

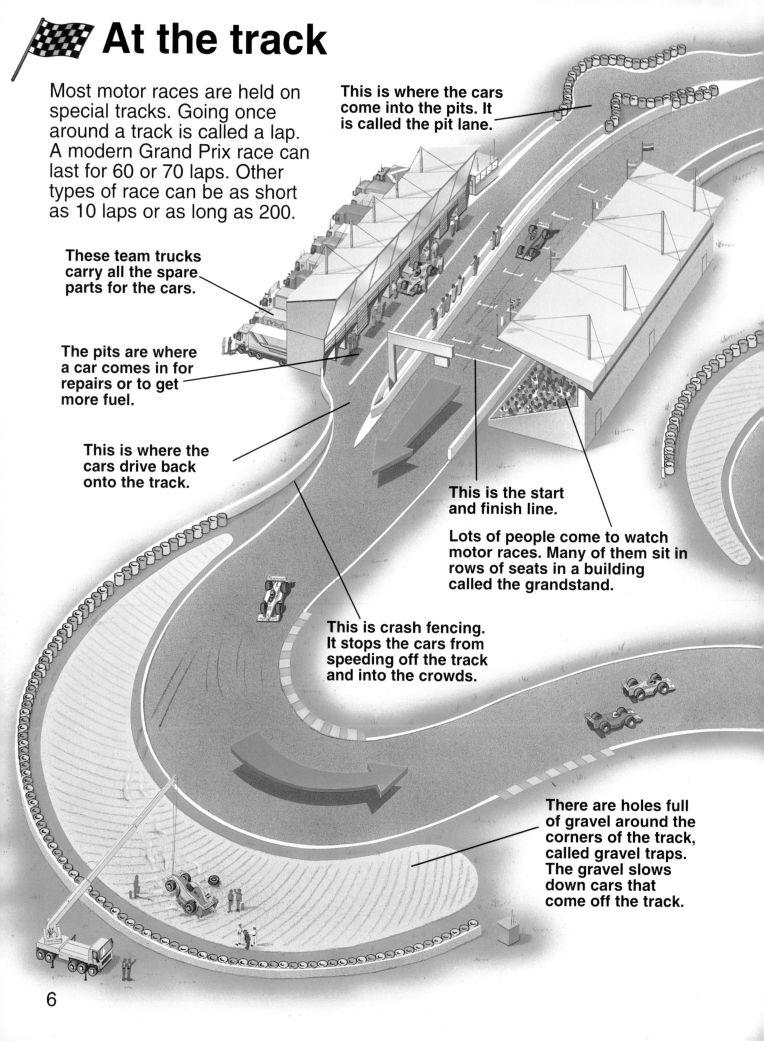

Most motor races are held on special tracks. Going once around a track is called a lap. A modern Grand Prix race can last for 60 or 70 laps. Other types of race can be as short as 10 laps or as long as 200.

This is where the cars come into the pits. It is called the pit lane.

These team trucks carry all the spare parts for the cars.

The pits are where a car comes in for repairs or to get more fuel.

This is where the cars drive back onto the track.

This is the start and finish line.

Lots of people come to watch motor races. Many of them sit in rows of seats in a building called the grandstand.

This is crash fencing. It stops the cars from speeding off the track and into the crowds.

There are holes full of gravel around the corners of the track, called gravel traps. The gravel slows down cars that come off the track.

## The starting grid

At the start of a race, the cars line up on a part of the track called the starting grid. The order the cars line up in is decided beforehand. There are painted marks on the grid to show where the cars start from.

The front place on the grid is called pole position.

## Marshals and flags

Marshals help make the race run smoothly. They report on drivers if they have cheated or caused a crash. Control flags are shown by marshals to warn drivers of danger. Here are some of them.

This flag tells drivers to stop overtaking on the track.

This tells drivers to go slowly to the pits. It is used when a race is being stopped.

This means that there is oil or water spilled on the track.

The chequered flag is waved as the winning car crosses the finish line.

Cranes around the track clear up any crashed cars.

These are stacks of old car tyres, roped together. They make up a strong but soft barrier to protect any cars that come off the track.

A hairpin bend is a very tight corner. The drivers have to slow down to a low speed to get around the corner safely.

A double bend in the track like this is called a chicane. Chicanes make drivers slow down.

# NASCAR racing

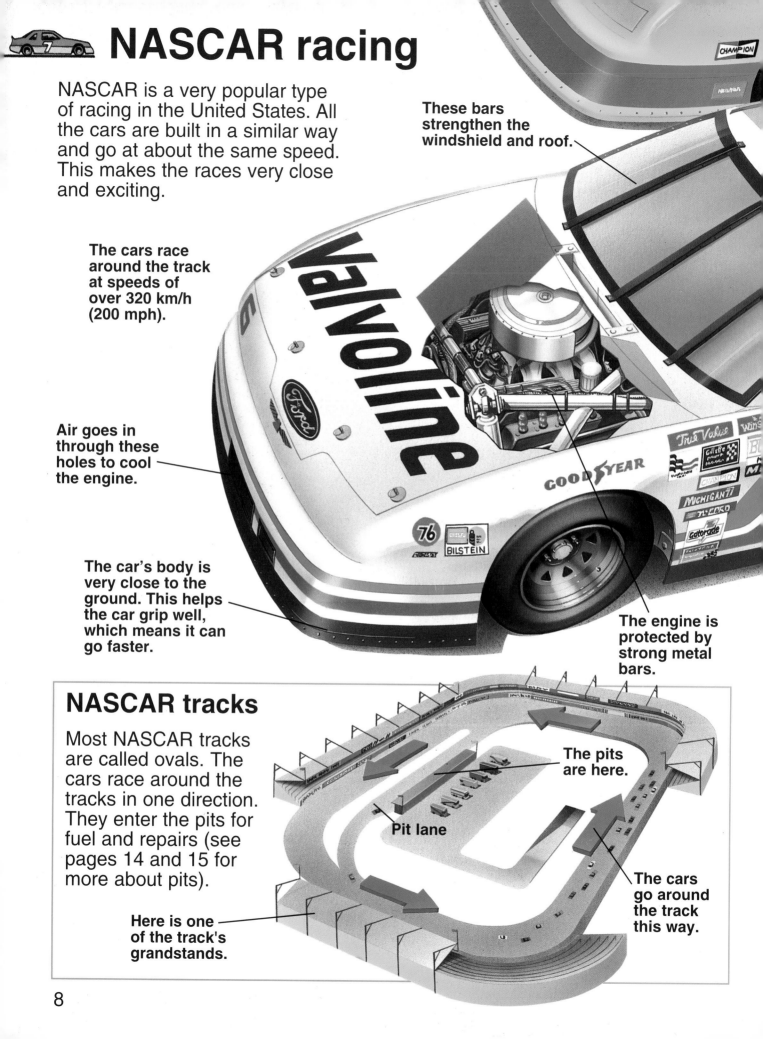

NASCAR is a very popular type of racing in the United States. All the cars are built in a similar way and go at about the same speed. This makes the races very close and exciting.

**These bars strengthen the windshield and roof.**

**The cars race around the track at speeds of over 320 km/h (200 mph).**

**Air goes in through these holes to cool the engine.**

**The car's body is very close to the ground. This helps the car grip well, which means it can go faster.**

**The engine is protected by strong metal bars.**

## NASCAR tracks

Most NASCAR tracks are called ovals. The cars race around the tracks in one direction. They enter the pits for fuel and repairs (see pages 14 and 15 for more about pits).

**The pits are here.**

**Pit lane**

**Here is one of the track's grandstands.**

**The cars go around the track this way.**

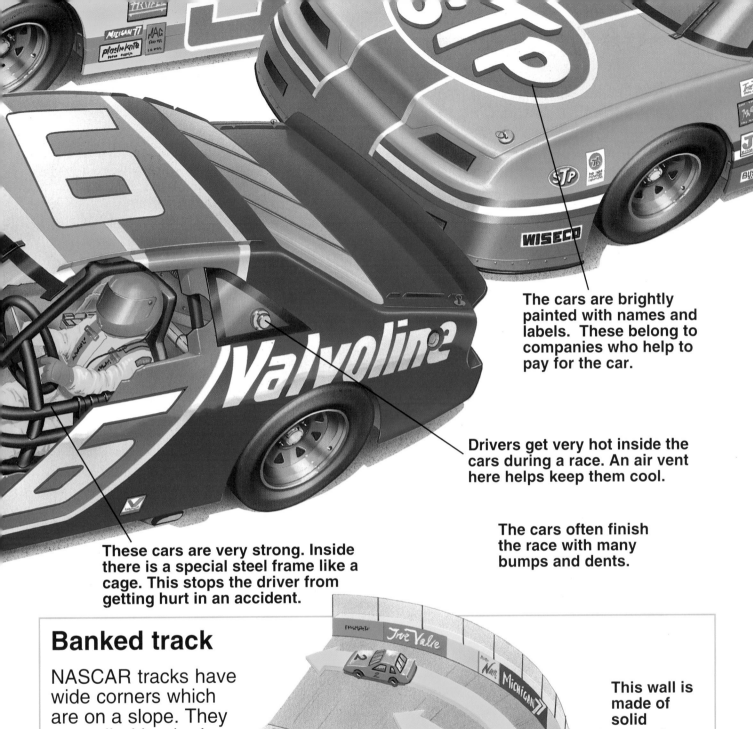

The cars are brightly painted with names and labels. These belong to companies who help to pay for the car.

Drivers get very hot inside the cars during a race. An air vent here helps keep them cool.

The cars often finish the race with many bumps and dents.

These cars are very strong. Inside there is a special steel frame like a cage. This stops the driver from getting hurt in an accident.

## Banked track

NASCAR tracks have wide corners which are on a slope. They are called banked curves.

Most of the bumps and crashes in a NASCAR race happen on the curves.

Drivers can choose to go around corners at a high, medium or low level.

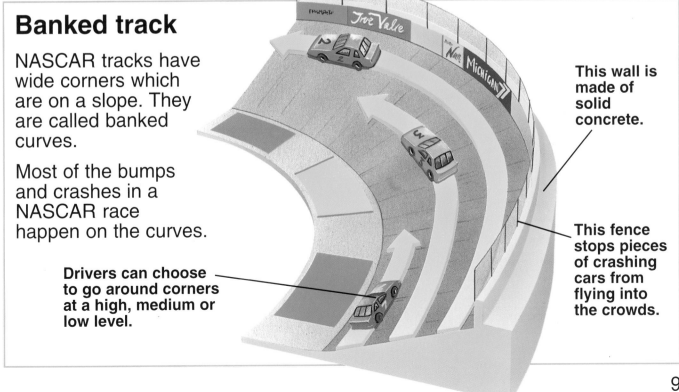

This wall is made of solid concrete.

This fence stops pieces of crashing cars from flying into the crowds.

# Rallying

Rally cars race along country tracks and sometimes on roads. They all follow the same route but start one after the other. They are carefully timed and the car with the fastest time is the winner.

Rallying is dangerous and the cars often crash and roll over.

A frame made of tubes of steel protects the people inside a rally car. It is called a roll cage.

## Rally cars

Rally cars are based on ordinary family cars. They are much tougher, though, and have extra strong bodies. They need these because the cars race over very rough courses with many bumps and dips.

These tyres are specially made to grip the rough tracks.

# Inside the rally car

The cockpit of a rally car has some extra equipment you would not find in an ordinary car.

These are called bucket seats. They grip the driver and co-driver and protect them from bumps.

This is the navigator or co-driver's seat. The co-driver helps the driver follow the correct route.

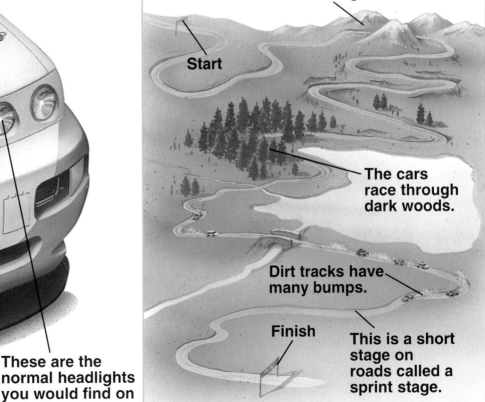

This special computer can work out how well the car is doing in the race.

The radio keeps the car in contact with its team of helpers.

Here you can see part of the roll cage.

These extra lights help the driver see bumps and bends in the road. These are very useful when rallying at night or through dark forests.

These are the normal headlights you would find on a family car.

# The rally

Rallies are made up of lots of parts called special stages. These test the car and driver in different ways.

The cars have to make many twists and turns on this mountain stage.

Start

The cars race through dark woods.

Dirt tracks have many bumps.

Finish

This is a short stage on roads called a sprint stage.

# Dragsters

Dragsters are cars which race a short distance along a straight track. They race in pairs against each other.

**A dragster spins its back wheels just before the start of a race. This is called burning out.**

**The car needs a fast start so the engine is warmed up before the race.**

**Burning out creates a lot of smoke.**

## Wheelie bars

A wheelie is when the front of a car lifts up into the air. Wheelies slow cars down. Some dragsters have a machine to stop them doing big wheelies. This is called a wheelie bar.

**Small wheel attached to back of car.**

Wheelie bar

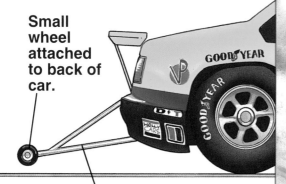

The wheelie bar helps stop the car from lifting up too much.

**Burning out makes the tyres hot and sticky. This helps the car grip the track.**

**The front wheels of dragsters are much smaller than the back wheels.**

## The drag strip

The track that these cars race along is called a drag strip. The strip is flat and straight. It is only 400m (¼ mile) long. The two cars that are going to race line up next to each other.

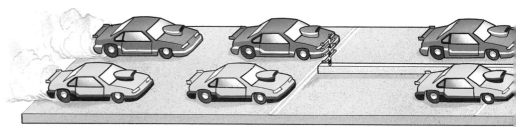

The cars burn out to build up power. Then they move to the start line and wait for the green light.

The cars start racing. The race is over very quickly. It will only last for five or six seconds.

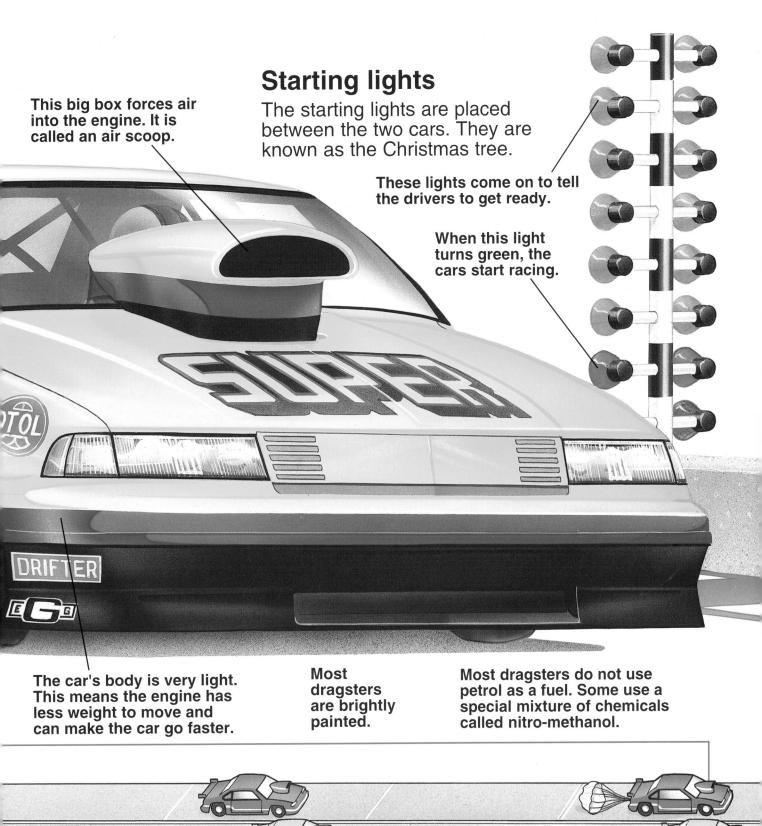

**This big box forces air into the engine. It is called an air scoop.**

## Starting lights

The starting lights are placed between the two cars. They are known as the Christmas tree.

**These lights come on to tell the drivers to get ready.**

**When this light turns green, the cars start racing.**

**The car's body is very light. This means the engine has less weight to move and can make the car go faster.**

**Most dragsters are brightly painted.**

**Most dragsters do not use petrol as a fuel. Some use a special mixture of chemicals called nitro-methanol.**

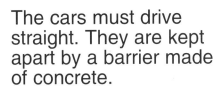

The cars must drive straight. They are kept apart by a barrier made of concrete.

Cars like these reach speeds as high as 320km/h (190mph) as they cross the finish line.

After finishing, the cars slow down. They use their brakes and sometimes a parachute.

# In the pits

In many types of race, cars are allowed to stop for help. The cars drive off the track and into the pits. There, people called mechanics repair the car as fast as they can. Repairs must be quick or the driver will get behind in the race.

**The fastest pit stops for a wheel change can take less than five seconds.**

## Changing tyres

Racing tyres wear out very quickly. Cars often come into the pits to change tyres.

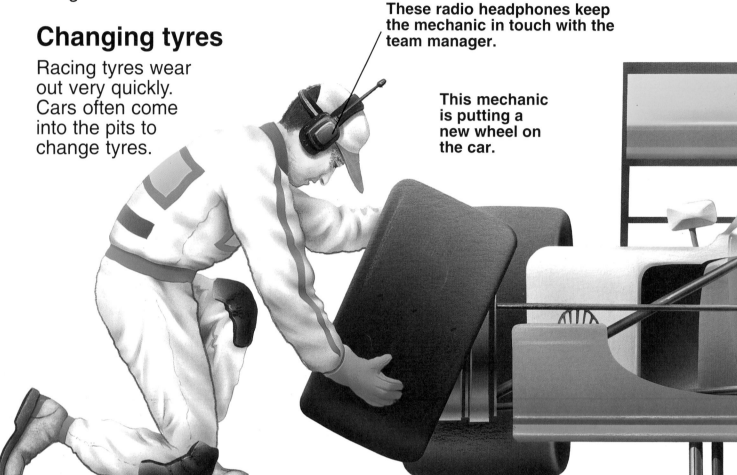

These radio headphones keep the mechanic in touch with the team manager.

This mechanic is putting a new wheel on the car.

## Pit boards

The pit board is held out over the track so that the driver can see it as he speeds past. It may tell the driver to come into the pits. It can also tell him how the car is doing in the race.

The top number shows where the driver is placed in the race. This car is first.

This shows the driver how many seconds he is in front of the car behind.

This is the number of laps the driver has already done.

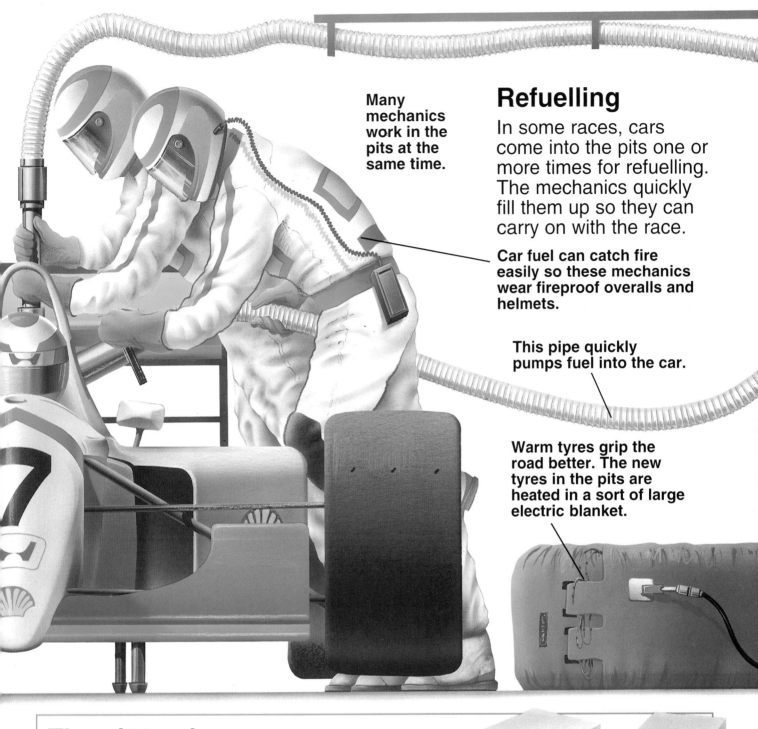

**Many mechanics work in the pits at the same time.**

# Refuelling

In some races, cars come into the pits one or more times for refuelling. The mechanics quickly fill them up so they can carry on with the race.

**Car fuel can catch fire easily so these mechanics wear fireproof overalls and helmets.**

**This pipe quickly pumps fuel into the car.**

**Warm tyres grip the road better. The new tyres in the pits are heated in a sort of large electric blanket.**

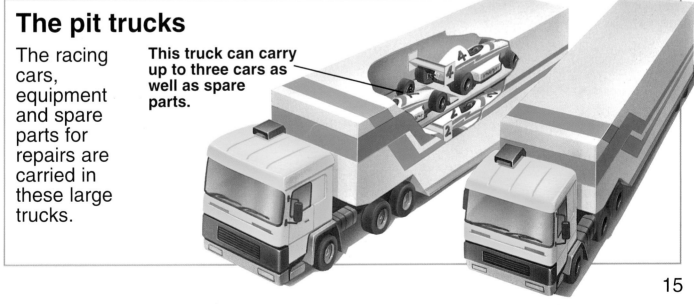

# The pit trucks

The racing cars, equipment and spare parts for repairs are carried in these large trucks.

**This truck can carry up to three cars as well as spare parts.**

# Learning to race

Racing is quite different from ordinary driving. Most people who want to race train at special schools. They have different lessons depending on the type of car they want to race.

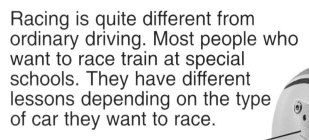

**Even though karts are not very powerful, the drivers must still wear crash helmets.**

**The engine on this kart is 10 times smaller than the engine in an ordinary family car.**

**Basic karts have a top speed of around 100km/h (60mph).**

**These wheels are only 20cm (8in) across.**

## Karting

Karts are the smallest racing cars. They are the first cars most people learn to race. Many famous rally and Grand Prix drivers first learned to drive in karts.

**Basic karts have no gears. They just have an accelerator pedal to go faster and a brake to slow down.**

## Saloon car

When you first learn to drive on a track, you have an instructor sitting beside you. The instructor drives first, showing you the safest way to take the car around the track.

**Learner racing driver**

**Instructor**

**The roll cage protects the driver and the instructor.**

**This learner driver has turned the car too fast. A wheel has lifted off the track.**

# Off-road racing

Racing across countryside where there is no track is called off-road racing. It teaches you to drive over muddy, bumpy and slippery ground. This is good practice for many other types of racing.

These bars protect the front of the car. They are called crash bars.

**This flap stops mud from flying off the wheels and onto the windows.**

**This car has chunky wheels which make it easier to drive through deep mud.**

# Single-seater racing

After lots of races in karts, a driver can try out a single-seater racing car.This is the first step to driving a real Grand Prix car.

**The driver sits in an open cockpit.**

**This metal hoop helps protect the driver if the car rolls over.**

**These cars can reach half the speed of a top Grand Prix racing car.**

# Indycars

Indycars look like Grand Prix cars but they are bigger and heavier. They race in the United States, Canada and Australia.

Indycars are named after the Indianapolis 500, the most famous race that they take part in. Indianapolis is the city in the United States where the race is held.

## Racing car wings

Some racing cars have wings. They use them in the opposite way to a plane. When air passes over a plane wing, it lifts the plane up.

Plane wing rises up.

Air

Racing cars turn the wings upside down. When air passes over the upside-down wing, it pushes the car down onto the track.

Wing pushes car down.

Air

Car grips the track

An Indy car has two of these wings, one at the back and one at the front.

Rear wing    Front wing

This part of the car is called an air scoop. It forces air onto the brakes to keep them cool.

These rods hold the wheel firmly. They are called suspension arms.

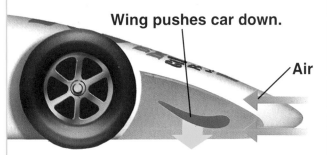

The body of an Indycar is very smooth. This helps the car go even faster.

## Different tyres

When wet, racing tracks are slippery. Tyres with lots of grooves help cars stick to the track. When the track is dry, the grooves slow the car down so smooth tyres called slicks are used instead.

Slick tyres

Wet weather tyres

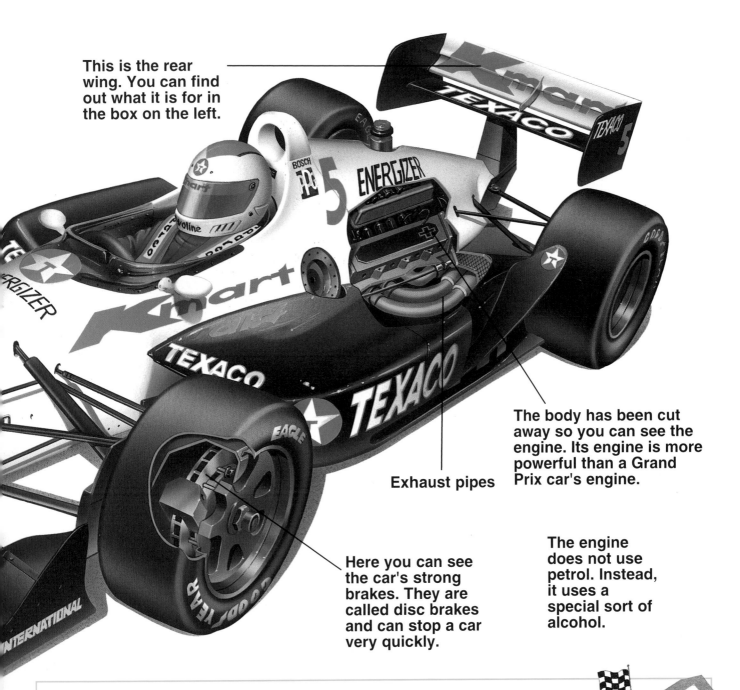

This is the rear wing. You can find out what it is for in the box on the left.

The body has been cut away so you can see the engine. Its engine is more powerful than a Grand Prix car's engine.

Exhaust pipes

The engine does not use petrol. Instead, it uses a special sort of alcohol.

Here you can see the car's strong brakes. They are called disc brakes and can stop a car very quickly.

## Races and tracks

Indycar races are often called '500s', because they are 500 miles (805km) long. Indycars sometimes use the same tracks as NASCAR racing cars (see pages 8 and 9).

Pit lane

This is the Molson Indy track in Canada.

Start and finish line.

It has twists and turns like a Grand Prix track.

# Monster racing cars

These amazing cars are pick-up trucks with many special features added. The cars are raised high off the ground so that they can drive over things in their way. They race in pairs, speeding over bumpy and muddy courses.

The car has many parts covered in a bright, shiny metal called chrome.

The cars have brightly painted bodies.

Power from the engine goes to the back and front wheels. This is called four-wheel drive.

These are called shock absorbers. They act like cushions as the car goes over bumps.

The car's wheels are huge. Each one is larger than a tall person.

Old, wrecked cars are put in the monster racer's way.

The drivers are very proud of their cars. In between races they keep them very clean.

One wheel and tyre weighs 440kg (1000lb).

## Monster crawler

This is like an ordinary monster racer but it does not have wheels. Instead it has tracks like a tank or a bulldozer.

The engine is under here. The biggest engines in these cars are over 15 times as powerful as an ordinary family car.

One litre of ordinary car fuel will drive monster racers only 300m. (That's about 1mile per gallon.)

These logs are all wired together.

## How high is a monster racer?

Monster racers are twice as high as an ordinary pick-up truck. They are over 3.5m (11ft) high.

This space in the car body is for a normal wheel. It is called the wheel arch.

These wheels come from massive farm vehicles.

This is an ordinary pick-up truck.

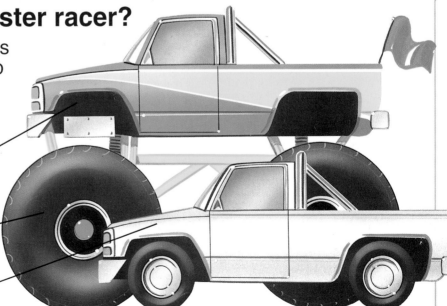

# Dirt track racers

Some tracks are made of dirt. The cars that race on them are called dirt track cars. Up to four of them race against each other at the same time. The big car you can see here is from the United States.

**Cars like this usually race on oval dirt tracks.**

## European stock cars

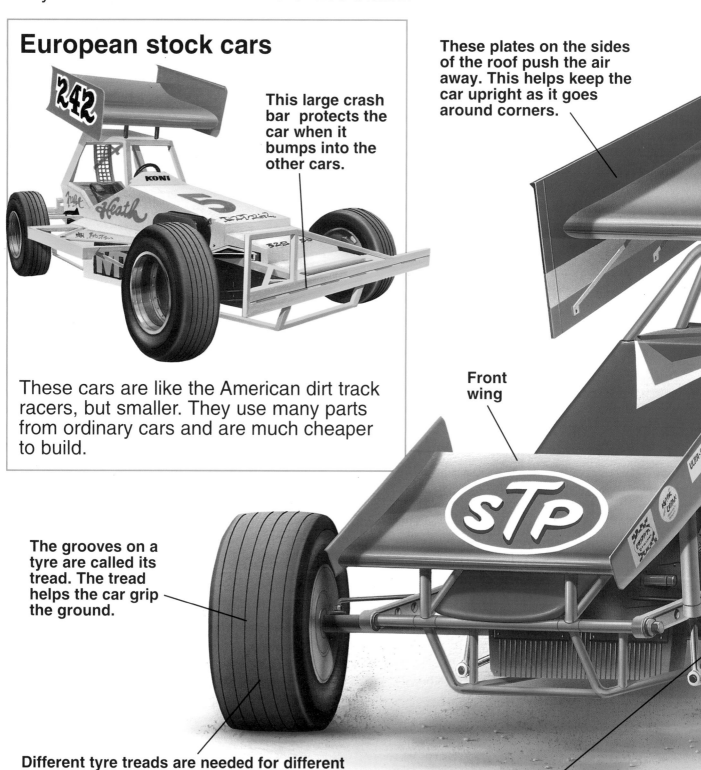

This large crash bar protects the car when it bumps into the other cars.

These plates on the sides of the roof push the air away. This helps keep the car upright as it goes around corners.

These cars are like the American dirt track racers, but smaller. They use many parts from ordinary cars and are much cheaper to build.

**Front wing**

The grooves on a tyre are called its tread. The tread helps the car grip the ground.

Different tyre treads are needed for different types of ground. On dirt tracks, tyres with a very deep tread are used.

This is the front axle. It joins the two front wheels together.

These are the names or labels of companies who have helped build or pay for the car.

The cockpit is open. The driver is protected by the bars of the roll cage.

The driver wears a set of straps called a racing harness.

The back wheels are very wide. This helps the driver control the car around corners.

## Turning corners

Turning corners as fast as possible is one of the most difficult parts of racing. Drivers must react quickly if anything goes wrong.

Yellow arrows show which way the car is moving.

The driver turns the wheels to get around the corner.

If the car is going too fast when it turns, the back wheels may swing to the side.

The driver must slide the back wheels to the other side to make the car point the right way again.

# Le Mans cars

One of the most famous races in the world is held at a race track near Le Mans in France. It lasts for 24 hours. The winner is the car which does the most laps in that time.

Le Mans cars are driven by teams of drivers. When one driver gets tired, another takes over.

The winning car will run at an average speed of over 210km/h (130mph) for the whole 24 hours.

This car is called a Porsche 962.

PORSCHE

Shell

BOSCH

DUNLOP

OXIDIZING AGENT

5

11

Shell

DUNLOP

BOSCH

This engine is eight times as powerful as the engine of an ordinary family car.

The body's shape lets the air flow over it easily. This helps the car go faster.

This car has a top speed of 400km/h (250mph).

## Old Le Mans cars

Cars have been racing at Le Mans since 1923. Cars made by Bentley, Ferrari, Ford, Jaguar and Mercedes have all won there.

This Bentley Speed Six won Le Mans in 1929 and 1930.

The Bentley carried a spare wheel on the side of its body.

# Porsche 911 Turbo

This is one of the most famous Le Mans cars. You sometimes see cars similar to this on the road.

This car can go from standing still to 100 km/h (60mph) in under six seconds.

**The Porsche 911 first raced at Le Mans in the 1960s and modern 911s still race there today.**

**The front lights are strong and bright as the car has to run all through the night.**

## Quick repairs

**The front part lifts off to show the front lights and wheels.**

**The back part lifts off to show the engine and gearbox.**

**This car is called a Jaguar XJ220C.**

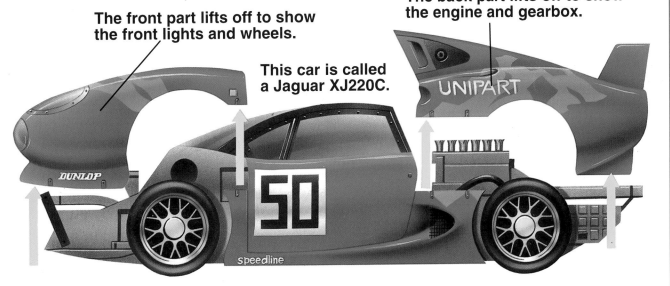

Le Mans cars often come in to the pits during the race. A car must be back on the track as soon as possible. To help the mechanics make the repairs quickly, a lot of the car's body lifts off in sections.

 # Desert rallying

Rallies are held all over the world. Some of the toughest rallies are through deserts.

**This is called an air intake. It allows air into the engine, which is in the back of the car.**

**Wipers keep sand off the windshield.**

**The space inside the car is taken up with a few spare parts, supplies and lots of water.**

**The car's co-driver tells the driver which way to go.**

**There are no fuel stations in the desert, so this car carries 350 litres (77 gallons) of fuel. That's over five times as much as a normal car.**

**Desert rallies are not races across flat sand like at a beach. Many parts of a desert race are up and down steep sand dunes and over rocky ground.**

**This part of the car is called a mudflap. It is made from tough plastic. It protects the underneath of the car from stones and small rocks flying off the wheels.**

# Desert racer

This is a French car called a Citroën ZX. It is racing through the Sahara Desert in North Africa.

**There are extra lights for rallying at night.**

MICH

**This sheet of tiny wire loops is called a net cover. It lets air in to help cool the car but stops stones from getting in.**

**The cars often break down. They have to be repaired on the way by the support team.**

# The support team

A desert rally team includes many vehicles other than the actual rally car. All of these help in some way. They are called support vehicles.

**Some big rally teams have a helicopter. It is used to spot any problems ahead of the rally car.**

**All the mechanics and other team members have to be looked after. This canteen van makes meals for everyone.**

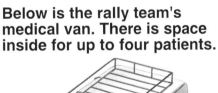

**Below is the rally team's medical van. There is space inside for up to four patients.**

**Above is the main service van. It contains many spare parts for the car.**

**This motorbike can pick up the driver and co-driver or pass messages to them if the radio breaks down.**

# Old racing cars

The very first car race was held in France in 1895. Since then, many types of cars have raced in lots of different competitions. Here you can see four of them.

## Bugatti T35

This French car first raced in 1924. It was very fast for its time. It had a top speed of 193km/h (120mph).

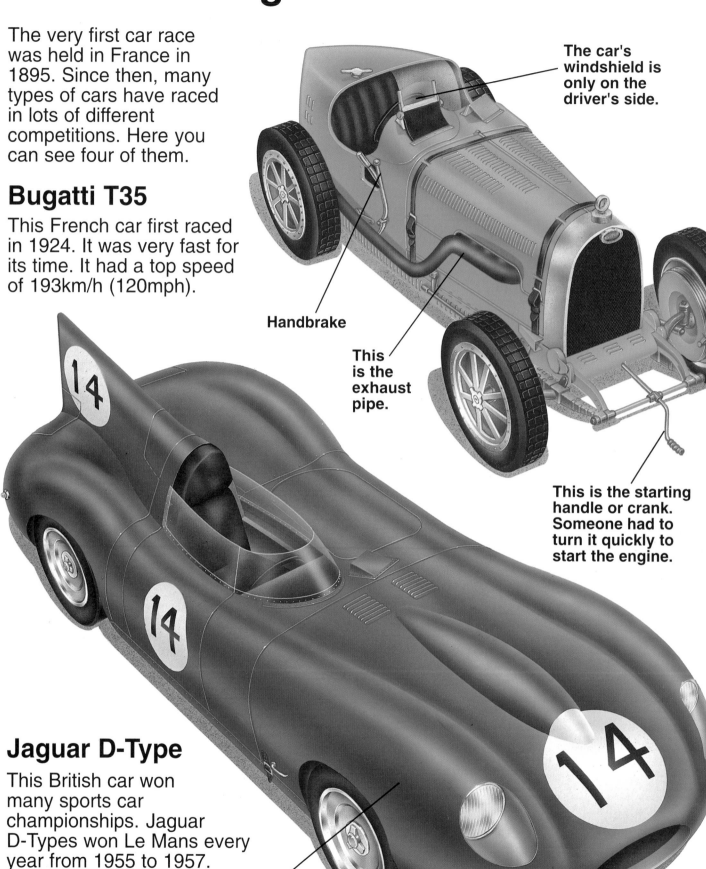

The car's windshield is only on the driver's side.

Handbrake

This is the exhaust pipe.

This is the starting handle or crank. Someone had to turn it quickly to start the engine.

## Jaguar D-Type

This British car won many sports car championships. Jaguar D-Types won Le Mans every year from 1955 to 1957.

To help it go faster, the car has a smooth body.

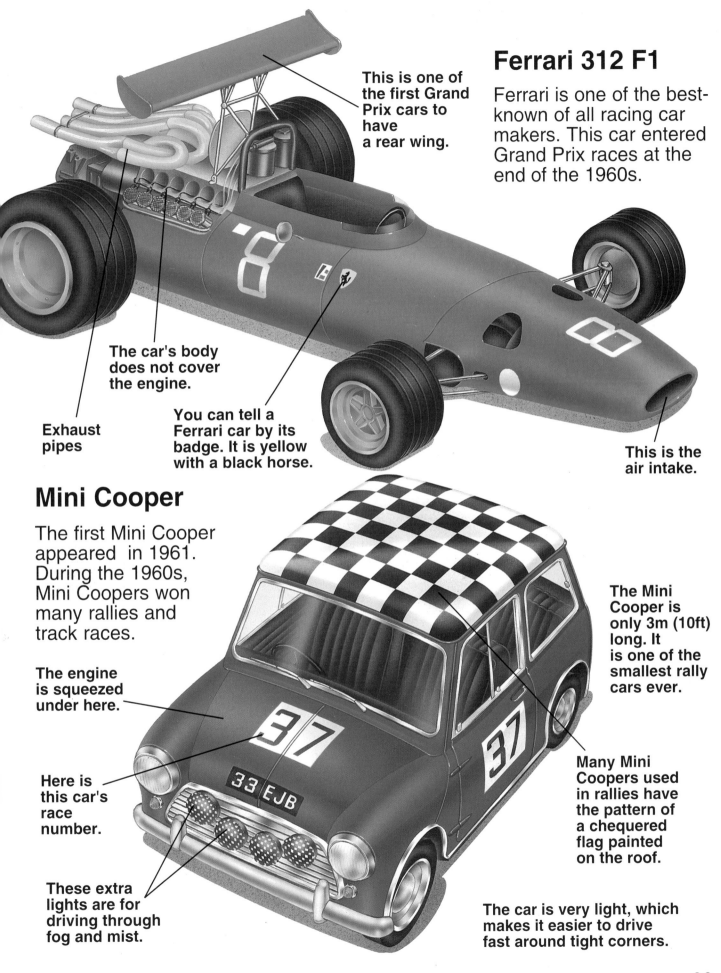

## Ferrari 312 F1

Ferrari is one of the best-known of all racing car makers. This car entered Grand Prix races at the end of the 1960s.

This is one of the first Grand Prix cars to have a rear wing.

The car's body does not cover the engine.

Exhaust pipes

You can tell a Ferrari car by its badge. It is yellow with a black horse.

This is the air intake.

## Mini Cooper

The first Mini Cooper appeared in 1961. During the 1960s, Mini Coopers won many rallies and track races.

The engine is squeezed under here.

The Mini Cooper is only 3m (10ft) long. It is one of the smallest rally cars ever.

Here is this car's race number.

33 EJB

Many Mini Coopers used in rallies have the pattern of a chequered flag painted on the roof.

These extra lights are for driving through fog and mist.

The car is very light, which makes it easier to drive fast around tight corners.

29

# Crazy racing cars

A few cars that are used for racing look very strange indeed. You can see some of them on this page.

**The roof of this car protects the driver if the car rolls over.**

**This strong plastic netting helps stop the driver from falling out.**

**These are normal road tyres.**

**This is called a nudge bar. It is like a strong bumper.**

## Dune buggy

Dune buggies race across sand and open ground. They are light and tough and are often built out of parts from old cars.

**This buggy uses lots of parts from a car called the Volkswagen Beetle.**

**The cars often roll over when they hit a high sand dune.**

## Cars in disguise

A Thunder Saloon is a racing car made out of an ordinary family saloon car with lots of things added. Extra parts are attached to its body, and an enormous, powerful engine is put in.

**This is a Vauxhall Calibra that has been turned into a Thunder Saloon.**

**The new engine is over five times as powerful as an ordinary car engine.**

Spare tyre

This is the exhaust pipe.

CNC

This is a normal Vauxhall Calibra.

Calibra

## Six-wheel racing cars

Today, all Grand Prix cars must have four wheels. A few years ago, though, some racing cars were made that had more than four wheels.

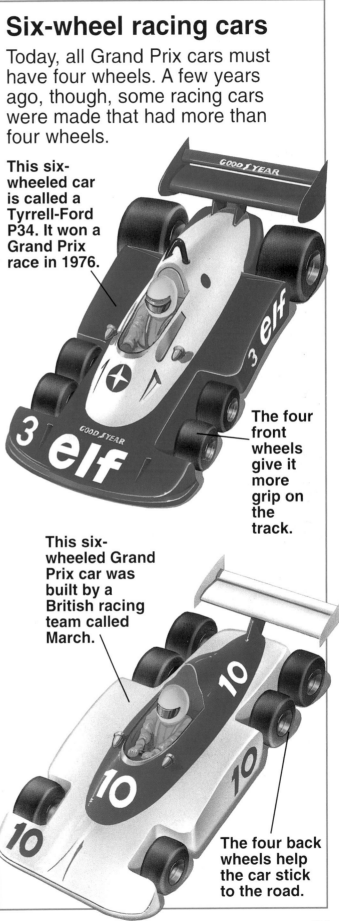

This six-wheeled car is called a Tyrrell-Ford P34. It won a Grand Prix race in 1976.

The four front wheels give it more grip on the track.

This six-wheeled Grand Prix car was built by a British racing team called March.

The four back wheels help the car stick to the road.

# Index

**With special thanks to Brands Hatch, Citroën UK, The Welsh Karting Centre and Valvoline (UK) Ltd.**